# Anything

## Is

# Possible

Thought–Provoking Quotes
to Inspire Your Mind

*Lorenzo Victory*

# ANYTHING IS POSSIBLE
## THOUGHT-PROVOKING QUOTES TO INSPIRE YOUR MIND

iUniverse books may be ordered through booksellers or by contacting:

iUniverse
1663 Liberty Drive
Bloomington, IN 47403
www.iuniverse.com
844-349-9409

ISBN: 978-1-4917-0471-4 (sc)
ISBN: 978-1-4917-0469-1 (e)

Library of Congress Control Number: 2013915056

Print information available on the last page.

iUniverse rev. date: 10/16/2020

I dedicate this book to my family and friends.

My whole life has been supported by a strong network of friends and family who have always been there for me during sickness and in health.

I also dedicate this book to those who struggle with any illness and to those who encounter any obstacles in their lives.

Lastly, I dedicate this book to those who will be inspired by it and who realize that *anything is possible*.

# Table of Contents

# Acknowledgments

I would like to thank my family for the love and support they have given me throughout my life. I would also like to thank my close friends for always being there for me. My mother, father, and sister have been wonderful my whole life and have always supported me—no matter what was occurring. I have been inspired by my mother and father. I have also been inspired by my sister and brother-in-law and, lastly, by my niece and nephew.

# *Introduction*

This book is based on my personal experiences in life. I have found that my messages of being confident and staying positive have helped others, and I'm confident they will help you too. I wrote this book to share my knowledge and experiences of setbacks and accomplishments. I hope it inspires you. This book is designed to help anyone who feels overwhelmed or uninspired, or who lacks confidence. I hope it will also lift your spirits and provide you with feel-good quotes and inspiring thoughts.

The following are inspirational, thought-provoking, positive messages and quotes that I have written. I write what I feel at the moment. I have endured many setbacks and obstacles throughout my life. I have overcome ailments and many hardships to get where I am. I have had a brain tumor, scoliosis, neurofibromatosis type 1 (NF 1), a heart attack, hydrocephalus, and more. I just retired as an officer at a major bank. I started as a teller and ended up as a manager. I worked as a banker for twenty-seven years. During my career, banking changed many times and we adapted to the changes. I lived with the motto "No excuses!" We all worked in a *no excuse* environment. We did our jobs. We all had our respective roles, and we all had accountability. We held ourselves liable for our conduct and our performance. When a task or assignment was not done, we learned not to blame others for our shortfalls. We took responsibility and answered to our managers. This is part of what helped shape me into the positive, confident person I have become.

I believe that anything is possible and that nothing can stand in the way of happiness and success. I want to share my messages and thoughts with the world. In this book I present my life—as seen through my eyes. I share my experiences and how I dealt with the good and the bad. I continue to find the strength to overcome daily issues that come with life. I feel very fortunate that I am able to write this book in order to show everyone that—no matter what your pain, issue, ailment, physical condition, or emotion is—you can decide the direction of your future. Poor health can take a toll on you. Sometimes it's unexpected, and sometimes it comes with age. Life can also throw curve balls at you. No matter what the issue is, the answer is *attitude*.

I began posting quotes on a social media site in late 2011. I received positive feedback nearly every time I posted a quote. All of the quotes are my original quotes. I felt inspired by the feedback I received when I wrote them. After careful consideration, I decided that others might benefit from reading my quotes and reading about my life and how I came to be the positive, confident, and caring person I am today.

My story starts with my life as a young child and the medical issues I faced. It also shows how I dealt with life and how I overcame those issues. I then list quotes based on different thoughts. I have divided the book into several topics and categories of my quotes and thoughts. My story's theme follows the quotes, and while the story starts off addressing that particular category, the story about my life also picks up where I left off when I write about the other topics. I have placed the quotes under the appropriate headings of five different categories. Although the story may tend to skip around a little, it all ties back into a continuing story that follows my theme. I hope my thoughts and quotes—along with my life experiences—inspire all who read them.

# Caring

This category and the quotes that follow are about caring. Below I share the beginning of my story. It sends a caring message followed by my quotes and thoughts that have a caring theme.

I started out caring about people early in my life. I was always able to make friends very easily and was never a selfish child. I always shared with friends and didn't mind if they didn't share back. My life started in Canada in April 1965. My parents migrated to Montreal, Canada, from Nazareth, Israel in 1963. My sister was born three years before me and was also born overseas. From the beginning, my sister and I played together daily and had a very close relationship. We often did many activities together. My father worked several jobs while my mother stayed home and took care of my sister and me. My mother would cook, clean, and take care of us while we played; we had fun hanging out with each other and with our friends. We moved to the United States in 1971 when I was six years old. My parents were sponsored by my uncle, who had moved from Nazareth first to Syracuse, New York.

Once I started going to school in New York, I met many children my age and made a lot of friends. We played outdoors a lot and always had things to keep us occupied: the playground near our apartment, a swimming pool, and a basketball court. Many of the children living in or near our apartment frequented the playground daily. We had a great time every day, and everyone mostly got along. At the time, I was unaware that there were some mean kids out there, and I didn't know anything about bullying, fighting, name-calling, or other things that I might encounter. I didn't realize that life wasn't always fun and games. Sometimes people can make life difficult—although not necessarily on purpose. I only knew happiness and that, for the most part, being a kid was fun. For the first couple of years, I thought this was the way life was for a kid in Syracuse. We went to school, had recess, went home, played, did homework, ate dinner, played more, slept, and repeated the cycle daily. The summer was even more enjoyable because we had longer days—and that meant more time to play. We didn't have any homework or many responsibilities in the summer.

After a couple of years, life—and people—started changing. I realized that some people weren't always nice and that some had a mean streak. I found that not all people were treated the same. I saw that some kids were mean to each other just because they didn't like the way other kids dressed or looked—or because they didn't like someone's hair. Some were made fun of because they were dark-skinned or too pale, or because they had red hair. Some kids made fun of other children just because they felt like it, and the worst part was that they actually seemed to enjoy it. They seemed to get satisfaction from watching other kids get sad and upset. I tried to stay away from kids like that; I avoided them. In fact, I was terrified of this type of kid. I felt it was only a matter of time before I would be the one getting picked on. I didn't know why, but I just had a feeling that soon other kids would pick on me. At the time, I didn't feel any different from any other kid—but I was short and dark-skinned, so I did my best not to draw attention to myself.

One day during recess I was looking at the face of a young African American girl when two kids were making fun of her because a bird had pooped on her arm. I was standing near her when it happened. The kids thought it was funny. They not only laughed, but they also drew attention to her by pointing and laughing; they made fun of her continuously until she cried. I distinctly remember thinking it was funny at first when the white bird poop landed on her arm, but when those kids brought her to tears, my mood suddenly shifted to empathy for her. I was only seven, but I felt horrible that she was being made fun of. She was crying because kids were laughing and pointing at her—not because the bird had pooped on her arm. Looking back, I found tremendous meaning in this. This was the start of something in my life that I knew would never end.

I cared for people. I felt empathy and sympathy for people. I carried that feeling throughout my life as a child and as an adult as well. As a young kid, I made friends with few people. I knew a lot of people and was friendly to all of them, but I made friends with only a few. It seemed that the kids I was friends with were also caring. Sometimes my friends were caring, and other times they weren't as caring as they should have been. Sometimes they would be the ones to poke fun at or pick on someone. It seemed that even the friendliest friend would poke fun at someone on occasion. Sometimes it would be that kid's turn to get picked on. I knew that most of this was horseplay and wasn't really serious bullying. That was true for the most part, but at certain times the true feelings and thoughts of some of my so-called friends would start to show. Some were not always the caring people I thought they were. This was especially true when it came to the way some treated *me*. I had friends whom I considered close—and mostly this was true—but on occasion even *my* friends would poke fun at me or lightly pick on me. Usually, it was harmless fun. At certain times, however, joking became a form of bullying. The primary reason for this was the way I looked. I was short, dark-skinned, and one of my nostrils was a little different from the other. I had light brown spots all over me. I looked "different" from the other kids. I had a hereditary disease I had been born with; I had been diagnosed with neurofibromatosis (NF type 1) at a very young age.

This is a neurological disorder that attacks your body in many ways. It begins by looking fairly innocent. Initially you develop light brown spots that resemble birthmarks on your body. Then you may start to develop small nodules or tumors all over your body. The number of tumors varies from person to person, but they can cover your whole body—including your torso, legs, arms, and face. At times, the disorder can be disfiguring. Some of these tumors are cancerous and some are benign. The nodules are connected to the nerves beneath the skin, and removing them can be troublesome or impossible; some can even grow back. There are usually few signs of these tumors until puberty. This is a genetic disease that affects approximately one in four thousand newborns.

Normally neurofibromatosis is a hereditary disorder, but my case was what they call a *spontaneous mutation* because no one in my family had this disease, yet I was born with it. I had early signs of this disease, but we never really knew what I had until later in my childhood. I had brown spots all over, and I was short with a larger-than-normal head. We just thought the brown spots were many birthmarks. I was an easy target for kids to tease me.

Once this disease started showing, suddenly I was the one who was teased. It was *me* who was getting called names—*me* who was getting pointed at. I was helpless as a young teen, and I didn't know what to do about it. I was a healthy teenage boy, and suddenly I had these things growing on my body. We saw doctors, but at the time they were not very knowledgeable about this disease. In fact, I had a nostril that wasn't shaped correctly; this was attributed to NF. When I was twelve, surgery was performed to correct the nostril and the end result made my nose and nostril worse. The NF returned and worsened, disfiguring my nose. When kids started making fun of me, I wasn't sure what to do about it—so I just let them. I didn't fight back. I didn't swear or run. I just took the abuse.

It wasn't just kids who stared, pointed, and made fun of me. Even adults made fun of me sometimes. Some adults would say things like, "Holy crap, what happened to your face?" Sometimes parents would tell their children, "Just don't look at him." I tried explaining my disease to people who said things. I told them that it wasn't a big deal and that it wasn't contagious, but some persisted in making fun of me or making a face with a disgusted look. Despite my answers, they continued making rude or insensitive comments. On occasion, I would get defensive and say that they couldn't handle having what I had.

I had never encountered this kind of ignorance before, so mostly I just sat there and took it. Some of these people were supposedly my friends, and some weren't. So, I did what I thought was best at the time. I built a wall up around me and became very quiet. I was bothered by this type of treatment, but I was not angry. Ironically, I did not feel the same way when a little child asked me what was wrong with my face. Or sometimes they would ask why I had bumps or mosquito bites all over my body. My answer to them was that I was born this way. Most kids would not ask further questions. Some would ask if the bumps were all over my body, and I would say "Yes." One boy asked if it hurt. I smiled and answered, "No, not really." As a young teen, I suddenly realized that the reason people made fun of me or asked me rude questions was not always because they felt like being mean. Sometimes it was because they were just curious but didn't know how to ask me about what they saw. Of course, some did it to be mean, but that was a small percentage.

I soon decided that shutting down and being quiet would not solve any problems. So I promised myself then that I would never let this disease break my mind or soul. I enjoyed being a kid. I liked people and liked having fun. I cared about people and realized that things sometimes don't go our way. I was determined to live my life and do my best, regardless of what life threw at me. I had this disorder and couldn't do anything about it; I was going to accept the fact that I had this disease. My parents always taught me to respect other people. They always said that the only thing that matters in life is *family,* because family will always be family. I hardly ever told my parents when kids teased or bullied me. I didn't want them feeling bad for me.

We are all born different and all look different. But we all have the same goals: to be happy, to dream, and to live out our dreams. Regardless of what I had, I decided to say, "Screw this disease—I'm living my life." I was determined to make friends, play with them, go to school, and do what every other kid did. At that very moment, I knew I was never going to pick on anyone or intentionally hurt anyone's feelings, *ever.* I realized there were all kinds of people in this world; we were all different yet all the same. I cared about people, and that was not going to change. Once you become a caring person, your whole attitude and demeanor toward the world changes.

# Caring Thoughts and Quotes

*I cannot stress enough the value of *true caring*. When you care about people, something magical happens. They change, you change, and society becomes a better place. Even better, selfishness disappears, and if you truly care about people, they become more caring toward others by example. Care in general—for *all* others—not just those you love. To make a difference, always care.

*Friendship—it's easy to be friends with people. It's easy to laugh with them. It's easy to hang out, eat together, and drink together. But all this is just being friends with someone.

*True friendship means sacrifice, risking one's life for the other, sincerity, and being there through good and bad times. True friendship has no prejudice and lasts until the end.

*Appreciate* is probably the most underused word in the English language. Just saying that word to someone goes a long way. Telling people that you appreciate what they do does wonders for their feelings and self-esteem. People can't read your mind. If you truly appreciate what someone did, you owe it to the person to let him or her know.

*For one day, make it your goal to make five people smile. You'll be amazed at how much better your day goes. You may just make someone's bad day much better.

*If your mind is clouded, then you must have doubted that you could free yourself from everything that bothers you-anything at all. It really can be true; all you have to do is call me.

*Reach out to someone close to your heart. Before your life comes undone, let someone do his or her part.

*People who really care about you care more about making you feel better than they do about anything else in the world at that moment.

*Help the needy if you can. Your heart will tell you how and when.

*A child's mind is precious. It's honest, blunt, funny, truthful, and without prejudice. Teach children to stay this way. Show them love and honesty. Teach them not to hate. The world needs more love— not hate. Children are always honest about their opinions.

*No matter what, always try living your life caring about others, especially those close to you. Care about their feelings, their health, their future, and their well-being. Don't worry if they care about you, because if you truly care, they will care for you too. Being selfish has no place in life. Take care of yourself too, but care for others *before* yourself. This will help make it easier for those you care about to achieve their dreams. Just being there is a great start.

*Sometimes just knowing that someone cares about you—and that he or she worries about you and tell you that—means the world. There are many ways to do this and many ways to say this. Tell people you care. Sure, they already know you do. But telling them works wonders! It's easy; just say, "I care."

*Sometimes we do or say something that we wish we could take back. Maybe you can. Maybe you can take a step back and try again.

Usually we let pride get in our way, or we don't know what to say. But don't ever let anything stand in the way of you being *you*. Be real, honest, and truthful—but never deceitful. Don't ever say anything bad or hurtful because it makes you feel good. Don't ever purposely hurt another's feelings. One day it might be too late to take it back. Always care, and you will never go wrong.

★A true friend will stand by you for who you are—and for no other reason.

★Why do some people seek to harm others or get joy out of spreading their anger? Why do some people allow themselves to be tormented by those people? And why is it that those people are never the ones being hurt? It's because they are tormented by *themselves*. They have been hurt, they usually don't like themselves, and they don't know how to treat others or how to behave. It's because they have never been loved, and no one has ever cared about them or taught them how to care. Care for other people and keep the cycle going.

★Try to be a good person. Try to be kind, funny, and caring. Try to feel and to be understanding. Try to be a good friend. Don't ever stop trying—*ever.*

★When you're not loved, you wither and die. Love someone, and you will save two lives.

★When a friend is in need, you don't have to be told. You can feel it. Be there for your friend, no matter what. Just listening and being there could make all the difference.

★Care for me and I'll care for you. It's that simple.

★Be the best. Be the best child. Be the best sibling. Be the best parent. Be the best uncle or aunt. Be the best relative. Be the best friend anyone could have. No matter what is going on in your life, you should always strive to be the best you can be.

*Struggle: All of us endure struggles and hardships sometimes. We may be able to handle it ourselves, or we may be lucky enough to have people in our lives to lean on. Others may not be able to handle struggle and may not have anyone to turn to. If you see or feel any of your friends of relatives struggling, offer to help—or just talk or listen. The suggestion alone may open the door to a solution that will help end their struggle. Use your strength to support others and help them to be struggle-free.

*Giving: This can be achieved several ways. Giving doesn't have to be monetary. It can mean listening, helping with a task, or donating time. Giving comes from the heart. Giving usually means caring. Always care.

*Togetherness: This means being with people you love and care for. Cherish the moment. No money in the world can replace it. With togetherness, you find success.

*Kindness is the greatest unselfish gesture one can give. Slowly, kindness can take over the world.

*I love, regardless. Do you?

*Priorities are not only meaningful to the person who makes them, but also to the people who care for them. Respect other people's priorities. You may just find you have something in common.

*Forgiveness is easy. Stubbornness is the hard part. Why work harder than you have to?

*When you care about someone, tell the person. Don't just assume he or she knows. Telling someone you care about him or her isn't hard. In fact, it's much harder when that person is no longer here.

*Kindness: Kindness is easy. It's simple. Of course we are kind to our family and friends. Yes, we are raised to say *please* and *thank you*. But when we deal with people who aren't related to us or aren't friends—are we always kind to them? Are we kind to the elderly, to teachers, to customers, or to your everyday average person? Being kind can change someone's mood and make his or her day brighter. Being kind can make good things happen. Being kind just makes you feel better. Being kind is just the right thing to do. Be kind today.

*To care for someone means more than being nice. To care for someone means to listen, to feel, and to be there to provide advice and knowledge based on experience—and to accept it if needed. It means to understand someone's point of view—to know that his or her feelings and thoughts count as much as yours do. To care for someone means to look out for that person's best interest. Be honest, truthful, and loving—and care for those you care about.

*Spend time with and appreciate your family. Care for your family. Lean on your family. Your family is the one thing you can count on for sure. But it all starts with you being there for them.

*When you care, you don't have to say it. You don't have to go out of your way to show it. It's usually the subtle things or the nonverbal actions that show it. It's usually just listening or just spending a little time with someone. Sometimes it's just being there regardless of how busy you are. When you care for someone, that person is never alone.

*Did you know that you don't have to be friends with someone or be related to him or her to make that person smile? Any interaction is an opportunity to make someone feel good. It doesn't take much. It could be a smile, a simple thank-you, or maybe a question like "How are you today?" We are so used to being busy with our own lives that we tend to forget that we cross paths with others daily. Everyone is out doing their thing, and we all deserve respect and kindness from each other. If done right, you may end up with someone thanking you even if the interaction didn't go the person's way. I know this is old, but treating others the way you want to be treated really works.

*Love bullies, because their families never taught them or showed them love. Teach them to love themselves and to respect others. It may be the only way they will stop bullying other kids.

*Words can be powerful. Words can inspire and enlighten. They can help build self-esteem and lift spirits. They can encourage and support. Words can be used constructively, but they can also be harmful. They can damage and hurt. They can be spiteful and mean or used to discourage. Words can be thoughtless and can damage someone's spirit. Words can be good or bad. Think before speaking. Choose your words carefully; they can last forever.

*It doesn't matter what other people think you are or what words they choose to hurt you. Since you are strong and confident, you can overcome any obstacle in your way—through your mind and attitude. Mental success is powerful and can break any attack on your spirit. Ignorance is weakness, but your perseverance will lead the way to a healthy state of mind and can help conquer other people's ignorance. The only winner will be *you*. Smile, because you are strong.

*It seems like a lot of people in this world feel entitled to things. People feel like it's their right to have certain things and to get certain good things. They're half-right. Everyone is entitled to get anything they want, but only if they earn it and work hard to get it. Nothing is free. Everything comes with a price, and the cost is sweat, effort, time, and passion. Only *then* are you entitled to get what you want.

# Mind

This category focuses on your mind being positive. The following story and quotes involve thinking and being positive—having a strong mind and thinking deeply.

I believe you can accomplish any task you face. I believe that the only thing that stands in your way is *you*. If you focus your attention on a particular task or goal, you can achieve it. It takes effort, drive, confidence, and—most importantly—the desire to do the task and the belief that you can do it effectively. It's pretty simple. Just use a common sales tactic. This is it—ready? It is highly likely that you can be successful in nearly every challenge if you *believe you can win*. Know what the challenge is. Know what you find difficult. Get to know everything about it and what it will take to get there to overcome this challenge. Study it like a book. Once you do, you will feel confident. It will become second nature. Don't be afraid; instead, trust that you will succeed.

We live in a world of change. Our lives change, our work atmosphere changes, people change, and we change. We need to adapt and not complain, and we must adjust to change.

When my body began changing at the age of twelve, I didn't panic. I learned to adapt to my condition and was content. When I was thirteen and in the eighth grade, I found out that my spine was not normal. During a school physical, I was found to have scoliosis, or curvature of the spine. I was immediately referred to a specialist. My parents and I met with an orthopedic doctor. My spine was so severely curved and abnormal that surgery was recommended. The doctor told us that it would be a very long and difficult surgery. My parents agreed to the surgery because the alternative could mean that I would end up severely disabled. I was asked how I felt about the surgery, and I really didn't have an opinion. I told the doctor and my parents that I would be okay with doing the surgery. During surgery, I had a long metal rod inserted in my spine to help straighten it. I had to spend an entire month in the hospital in a city an hour and a half from my home. My mother rented an apartment for the month near the hospital and was by my side daily. Many times she would make home-prepared food in the apartment and bring it to me to eat instead of the hospital food.

My surgery was painful, and they had to immobilize me so that my spine would stay straight. I had to spend several days in traction. It was not very pleasant, and it left strap marks all over my body. There was no bed for me to sleep on and no pillow. After a month in the hospital, I was fitted for a body cast that went from my hips to my neck. It looked like a vest. There were no arms, so it was like a permanent sleeveless jacket. There was a hole cut out for my stomach, and the cast was a tight fit. I had to wear this cast for eight months. It probably weighed twenty to twenty-five pounds. My parents rented a hospital bed for me, and it was placed in the family room because going up and down stairs was a challenge. I spent eight months unable to shower, and bathing was a challenge. I wasn't able to attend school, so I was tutored at home for the entire ninth grade. The tutor would come twice a week to teach and provide me with lessons and tests.

This spinal disorder was attributed to my disease, neurofibromatosis (NF). NF was my base disease, and many of my ailments resulted from it. When I first heard the news about my back, I was concerned, but I wasn't worried. I definitely was not sure what to expect. I was told that my doctor was the best around, that he had performed this surgery many times, and that I didn't need to worry. Well, naturally, my mother and father were *very* worried. But in the end, they were right. The surgery was a success, and although it took many months to recover, my back healed very well. This was just the beginning of my medical issues, however.

I went back to school the following year and had normal sophomore, junior, and senior years of high school. My NF progressed, however, and nodules continued to grow on my body and face. This happened slowly and wasn't too noticeable. I was fortunate to make friends with several people, and my teachers liked me, but I was subjected to occasional teasing or bullying by some kids. When I graduated from high school, I went on to community college and studied criminal justice. I wasn't entirely sure what I wanted to do, but being a police officer was one interest. In the meantime, I accepted a job at a bank as a teller so I had time to figure out my future.

When I was twenty years old and after college, I started getting headaches. Some were unbearable, while others were tolerable. I knew something wasn't normal. Aspirin didn't help. I went to the doctor a few times but got no answers. I thought that maybe it was all in my head and that there was nothing wrong with me. My sister kept after me to see a specialist. I was stubborn and felt that I was okay; I didn't want to see any special doctors. After a while, the pain worsened to the point where it was sharp and very uncomfortable, so I gave in and went to a doctor—only to find out that what I was feeling was much more than a headache. Some tests were ordered. I was put in a very large, round cylinder-type X-ray machine called a CAT scan machine. After a CAT scan of my head, it was revealed that I had a brain tumor about the size of a half dollar.

Once again, the doctor consulted with my parents and me. They told me everything would be okay and that I was in good hands with one of the top neurological surgeons in the state; they said I should trust the doctor and his opinion. The doctor's opinion was that I needed brain surgery. I was a little confused because the doctor was using medical terms that I had never heard before. My parents were very concerned. We asked for alternatives to surgery but were told that there really weren't any. The tumor was large and the doctor wasn't sure if I had been born with the tumor, or if it had been there a very short time. We didn't have time to watch it grow more. It was already too large. We all believed the surgeon was right, that his recommendation was correct, and that he knew what he was talking about. Sure, there was a huge risk—sure, it could have been cancer. But if there was one thing we could count on, it was that I needed the surgery. So we agreed.

This surgery required that I miss work for several months. I had just barely started working at the bank, but that was secondary at the moment. I mentally prepared myself for a long road. After a few more consultations and several more CAT scans, I was prepared to have the surgery to remove this massive tumor. Prior to my surgery, I met with six or seven doctors who would be involved in my surgery. Most would assist the surgeon, and some would observe and stand by in case they were needed. I was a little nervous that this procedure was huge and that so many doctors were involved.

After about eight or nine hours of surgery, I was sent to the recovery room. According to the doctor, the surgery went well. I received about thirty staples in my head to heal my scalp. My tumor was removed and sent for a biopsy. I was fortunate enough for the tumor to be benign. Although I was a little nervous as a young man, I was confident that I had a great doctor and I never really feared that the surgery would not go well. The doctor had so much confidence that it was hard to believe that the surgery *wouldn't* go well. His positivity and personality were amazing. I believed this surgery would go well—as I had believed in my spinal surgery—and it *did*.

I strongly believe that you have to believe and be confident that things in life will be okay. You must have confidence in your life, and you have to accept that certain things are going to happen to you and that you cannot control these things. What you *can* do, however, is control how you react to those things and understand that our reaction can and will control the outcome. We are all born with the ability to be confident. What we must do is believe in ourselves always, and know that we have more control over our lives when our attitude is positive.

There is solid evidence that belief, confidence, and not worrying are powerful tools to healing, both mentally and spiritually. Your mind is a powerful tool in determining the outcome of many situations in life, use it to your advantage. My surgeon had a quality about him that just exploded confidence and belief. He had such a positive attitude that I am convinced that his positivity carried over into me. I sincerely believe that my mind, my confidence, and my lack of fear played important roles in my recovery.

# Mind-Provoking Quotes

*Life is confusing. Finding all the answers is impossible. Don't try to figure it all out. Most answers are already known to you; you just have to discover them. Other answers remain unexplained, but they all serve a purpose.

*Decisions: What you decide has a lot to do with the next step in your life. In fact, it could have a lot to do with other people's lives. Decisions are critical to your future. Good decisions lead to good things ahead. Bad decisions lead to extra work, disappointment, and time wasted fixing the mistake. We will all make wrong decisions and choices, but don't make wrong decisions because it's the easy way out. Good decisions don't always mean it's going be easy, but in the long run they will save you a lot of energy and work. You will know when the choice doesn't feel right. Don't make the wrong decisions on purpose.

*Guess: Okay, so no one really knows what lies ahead. Sure, some people claim to know, and some pretend to know. The best you can do is *guess*, but what matters is what you do before that guess. Setting yourself up for success by doing proactive things will help make that guess easier. Doing the right tasks and preparatory work can help make that guess more realistic. You may be able to guess your future. Can you make the right guess?

*Realize what it means to realize what it meant.

★Strive, work hard, concentrate, and use all the effort needed. No matter what the task is, use all your smarts and knowledge; desire to finish that project, assignment, or chore. Do it right, do it strong, and do it now. Don't waste your energy and have to repeat it.

★Invent: Imagine what you can create if you think. Imagine the world without inventions. No idea is impossible. We need smart thinkers. Make your contribution. Always think and imagine and be part of history. The world is waiting.

★Think often, think big, and think ahead. The moment you stop thinking, you will have to think your way out of it. So, always *think*.

★Frustration happens to everyone. You deal with it. Speak your mind, and then forgive and forget. Then sleep. It's the only way, because tomorrow is another day.

★Forget resolutions and promises. Talk is cheap. Just try to be a better person; just do better things. Take care of yourself and follow your dreams. Only *you* can make the changes needed.

★Close your eyes and sleep, knowing that tomorrow is a new day. Do good things with the first day of the rest of your life. Make it count.

★Knowledge: It isn't about the amount of information you have learned. It isn't about the number of books you've read. It isn't about all the certifications, licenses, or degrees you've earned. Knowledge is about how you have *applied* what you've read and learned in life. It's also about using what you learned to create new ways to do things—and helping to pass your knowledge on.

★Life: It's like this. You wake up and decide what your day is going to be like. Everything you encounter is the result of other people deciding what *their* days would be like. Someone else's day doesn't have to affect your day, or maybe it does (if it's positive). See, the world is full of opportunity, and interacting with the right people can help you achieve wonders. Sure, you can reach your goals on your own, but having good people in the right places is most important and makes reaching your goals that much easier. Don't ever let other people decide your future, but let the right people help.

*Drama, jealousy, and hate are all bad things. Drama is meant for theater, not to create trouble. Hate isn't meant to be used, *ever*, and jealousy is just someone's way of saying that he or she doesn't feel like working hard enough to get what he or she is jealous of. These three things should never be part of anyone's life.

*I love sunny days. You can open the windows. You can wash your car (or truck, motorcycle, horse, or even your camel!). It's funny how nice weather can make people feel better, cheer them up, or make them smile. When the weather is cold, gloomy, and rainy, many people tend to be miserable, unhappy, and generally not in a good mood. Regardless of the weather, always try to be happy. Always be good to people despite things happening in your life that you can't control. If you concentrate on being good to everyone you encounter, it will become part of you. And karma has a funny way of working. It may not be perfect, but good karma is better than bad karma any day!

*Work hard, be busy, fight, fight, fight, be crazy.
Passion is the way to get more out of less.
Nothing gets done when you're lazy.
Loving what you do will lead to success.

*When it comes down to it, life is like a roller coaster. Up and down, round and round, twists and turns. True friends and education, patience, love, trust, and honesty are the glue that keeps you stuck on top longer than the wild ride. It loosens up once in a while, and off you go on the ride. But the stronger the bond is, the longer you stay on top of the world.

*Look at your friends and family, and be thankful that you have people to be thankful for. Don't complain about each other; at least you're not alone.

*Life is incredible. Thinking that it's not is also incredible. There are so many twists and turns in life, and everything happens for a reason.

*Think of all the people you love and all the people who have been a positive influence in your life. Then think of all the opportunities you have had. Think of all the happiness you have felt—and the sadness. Think of the times you have been mad and glad. Think about when you were young and all the good times you had. Then think of all your loved ones. Also, think about what life might be like in the future. Now, what would you think of if you had never been born? Be thankful you are alive to even *think*.

*Ambition is the beginning of the end result. Without ambition, nothing is possible—except lack of success.

*Always remember that your life is remembered for how you lived, not whom you lived with, how much money you had, nor what possessions you had—but for *how* you lived your life and who you were as a person.

*Think deeply about people you love and care for before those people think deeply about someone else.

*Patience is a learned skill that shows love and caring. Impatience is also a learned skill that is passed on to those we love, making them impatient. Always be patient and make your life simpler.

★Giving good advice is a gift better than the advice itself. Be there for someone.

★You never know what you can do until you start believing. Success or failure is your choice.

★When you're busy, life is crazy. When you're not busy, you go crazy.

★Work with what you have. Don't give up hope just because you feel hopeless. There is always a way to reach your goal. It may take more time or seem unreachable, but you will never reach your goal if you give up. We all have what it takes to get what we need. We need to use what we have in order to get there.

★Ambition: Without it, you're not motivated. You have no inner desire to succeed. With ambition, you can make things happen. You have self-confidence. Your goals suddenly seem and *are* attainable. Anything becomes possible. Ambition is the key to achieving a goal. What is your ambition? Set your sights on your goals. Have the ambition to follow through to the end, and never stop no matter what happens until you reach your goal. It could take a long time to succeed, but once you get there you will be rewarded with the best feeling in the world.

★*Plan* is a very important word. We all must have some kind of plan. It's difficult to be happy or successful without any type of plan in mind. It sets things in motion. Planning gives you things to look forward to and gives you a reason to look forward to those things. Plan things out first; then follow the steps to reach your goal. Without a plan, you may get lost.

★Great things start with great minds. Great days start with great attitudes. Think great today!

*Envision: All great ideas, goals, and inventions start with envisioning them first. You must imagine and think into the future. Being successful in your life depends greatly on mentally focusing on your goals and picturing them being realized. Then make them a reality by following the path to get you there. You will find the way. Only then can goals and great ideas become a reality. Without this, we may never achieve greatness.

*True friendship never needs a definition.

*Powerful words: Words are very powerful. They can encourage and inspire. They can destroy and hurt. They can make someone smile or make someone cry. When used in the right manner, they can make someone think or dream. Words are very meaningful, so be aware of what you say. You may not have bad intentions, but words often speak louder than you think. Speak from your heart. Think before you speak. Listen, inspire, encourage, advise, and let your words have a positive meaning.

*Creativity: It's different, it's original, and it also adds value. It's *you*. Be creative and contribute to our future.

*Do what you love—no exceptions.

*Trust is a very important part of everyone's life. To put it simply, trust is earned and trust is given. Never underestimate the power of trust. The bond of trust is strong. Once broken, it will never be the same.

*Defeat* is a very powerful word. The meaning varies depending on how it's used. To *defeat* means to conquer. But to *be defeated* means to fail. There are many times that we will feel defeated in life. We will feel helpless and without hope. We may even lose at times. But don't let this stop you from fighting. Don't let it prevent you from striving hard to overcome obstacles you face. Reach inside and use that strength and desire to succeed to crush, defeat, and be victorious. Don't let defeat beat you.

*When you work all your life, does it matter what you did for a living? Is the job you had more important than the job you did? There are many job titles. Many people do similar jobs. What really matters is *how* you performed your job, how you treated people, and the heart that you put into your job. Passion, personality, and dedication separate an employee who is remembered from one who is easily forgotten. This also applies to self-employed people. Honesty, integrity, and lots of blood, sweat, and tears are the key ingredients to being known as a great business owner. No matter what you do for a living, do your best every day.

*Choose the way you live your life. Everyone has to. If you aren't happy, choose another way. If you are happy, you have made wise choices.

*A blind person who looks forward to his or her future has better vision than most people with 20/20 eyesight.

*A friend is someone whom you never have to question if he or she is a friend.

*Life doesn't become important to some people until they realize too late that their lives are important to others. Make your life count.

*Never question your ability to overcome obstacles in your life. Question your inability to overcome these obstacles.

*The ability to push forward is a God-given strength that we all have. Never give up on anything. Never settle for less than you desire. Never let any event prevent you from fulfilling your dreams and goals. Push forward through all your obstacles, and you will be rewarded with success. We all have the ability, but do we all have the heart and desire?

*He who grows his mind grows his potential. He who grows his potential grows his contribution to the world.

*Stand up: This has a few meanings, but they are all positive. Stand up and be heard. Speak your mind. Stand up and defend those who cannot defend themselves. Stand up and take care of those you love. Stand up for what you believe in. Most importantly, stand up and be honorable. Always be a *stand-up person*.

*You matter. You count. You are worth just as much as every other person on earth. Believe in yourself, be strong, move forward—not backward—and learn from your mistakes. Never give up. Your idea could be the next great idea to help advance mankind. Never give up on your dreams. To accomplish your goal, you must do something about it. Unleash your passion.

*Be strong and always be who you are. You may encounter jealousy. People may try to trick you into a false relationship. Never change your character or your love for others, and you will prosper. Know when it's time to move on. In time, you will find the perfect person who appreciates you for who you are—not for *what* you are.

*Greatness comes from action, not inaction. It comes from leading the way. Greatness comes from being brave and overcoming hardship. It is being great at what you do, loving what you do, and struggling through what you do so others may benefit. Greatness is being kind, caring, and nonjudgmental. Greatness comes in many forms, but it is rarely about you. It's about what you can do for others.

*Your desire to do well must be followed by your effort to do well.

*When things don't go your way, don't ask why. Try to understand why, and when things go your way, don't just be happy. Know *why* you're happy.

*Follow your dreams. Somewhere along the way, you might just find out what you really want in life.

*No one can walk in your shoes unless they tie the laces themselves.

*Your future depends on the present. It's much easier to stay on the path than it is to change your past. Hard work and getting good advice should guide you. Don't be afraid to do either.

*Life is precious; we all live for a purpose. Our purpose is not to live, wondering what life is all about. Our purpose is to exist with each other, to love each other, and to find our way to happiness by doing the right things in life. We exist to teach our children the way to success and happiness by working hard, educating ourselves, respecting others, and always striving to be our best—while always remembering where we came from. There is nothing wrong with being highly successful and having a high net worth, a big beautiful home, and a wonderful family. But we need our kids and young people to realize that they are extremely important to the future of our existence and that hard work and being motivated and confident is how they are going to succeed. They must believe that they exist because we need them. We need to focus our attention more on their lives and how they are going to succeed. We need to encourage, inspire, and challenge the kids of today and give them self-worth. Only then can we make them believe that they are important and needed by all of us.

*Wisdom: Wisdom is not the state of being smart or knowing all the answers. Wisdom isn't even always knowing what to do. Wisdom is experience, knowledge, and understanding—all combined. Wisdom is not taught; it's shared—but it's only heard by those who seek it. Will you know wisdom when you hear it?

*We have never really lived life until we have loved our lives and those in it. Our lives only exist to those whom we have touched. Life is short. Make every moment count.

*Raise your head up. Be proud of who you are. Set your goals high. There isn't anything that cannot be done. No one has ever accomplished a goal without heart, passion, and effort.

*Proud: Be proud for what you believe in. Be proud of your job. Be proud of your goals. Be proud of your family. Be proud of your friends. Most importantly, be proud of making the decisions to change what you're *not* proud of. We all need one or two changes to make our lives better, healthier, or happier. Recognize, change, and implement—and be *proud.*

*Motivation: We all need it. We have all given it to others. We all have it inside of us, but not all of us use it on ourselves. Self-motivation isn't easy, but it's critical in achieving nearly any task. Some are motivated to work out, and some are motivated to better their career and life. Some are motivated to try to be a better person. Motivating yourself is difficult but becomes easier the more you do it. The reward is worth the time spent. We all know when we need to be motivated. If you find it difficult to motivate yourself, ask a friend for help. Don't stop at one task. Motivate yourself often!

*Be proud: If you know you have tried your best, be proud. If you have loved without prejudice, be proud. If you care about others, be proud. If you struggle but refuse to give up, be proud. If you have worked hard to reach your goal and you've reached it, be proud. If you are hesitant to give it your best shot, don't be; give it your all, and *be proud.*

\*Growth is measured by how much you have changed for the better as a person. We all have room to grow.

\*If you could inspire someone, how would you do it? We all have what it takes to inspire. We just have to invest the time. Inspire someone and watch that person's world grow.

\*Know what's right and do what's right. Inspire others by taking the lead. Always lead by example.

\*Forget the past. It's the *present* that counts. We have all made mistakes in our lives. Focus on the positives and what it will take to be successful. Not making the same mistake twice will make our future outlook bright. Failure is only failure if you fail to try again.

\*When you need someone to lean on, ironically, you are usually led to the person who needs *you* too. It's not the advice or answers that help you through your situation. It's the fact that he or she *listened*. Never take life on alone. Reach out to those you care about, and you will be cared for too. Your heart will tell you who. You may just get what you seek.

\*Family time is fun. Family time is great. Family time can be boring. Family time can drive you crazy. Family time can be eventful or uneventful. Most of all, family time is amazing. You only have one family and life is short. Make time for family time.

\*When you feel powerless and like you are in limbo, know that you are powerful and that only you can alter that. Nothing else can. We can all get a little overwhelmed at times, but you are capable of dealing with anything. Know that you can and you will.

\*You are empowered to do whatever your heart desires. Be prepared to take the necessary steps, or be ready to deal with the consequences.

★Make friends, make sense, make smiles, make goals, make dreams, make peace, and make love. Whatever you do, make it happen.

★Make your dreams a reality. You hold the handbook; in fact, we *all* do. Your choice is to use it.

★If life is meant to be fantastic, shouldn't we all be millionaires? Life is what you make it, and you can actually be a millionaire without being rich.

★Every day of your life is a new beginning. Take advantage of every moment. It's never too late to start your life right. Do it every day.

★Enthusiasm: It's much easier to have enthusiasm when you're genuinely enthusiastic. Be positive and stay positive. The end result will be positive.

★If hate is powerful, how do we beat it? We beat it by making it weak, and we weaken it with love. We love each other regardless of our differences. And the only thing we hate is *hate.*

★Doing what you want is only a good thing when what you want is truly a good thing.

★Your mental health depends on your attitude. Caring is healthy; love is healthy. Having a positive attitude is healthy. Being confident is healthy. Believing in yourself and your capabilities builds self-esteem, which is very healthy.

★You hold the key to happiness in your life. While one may *seem* to be happy, it may actually be an escape from reality in disguise. Happiness is family. Happiness is caring and love. Know when to recognize this. Happiness is not running wild without a care.

Happiness is responsibility and structure. Once you have mastered this, you can truly be happy.

★Your life is meaningful.
Your thoughts are meaningful. Your actions are meaningful. Your goals are meaningful. The question is—
Do you live your life well?
Are your thoughts good?
Are your actions good?
Are your goals good?
If you do anything in life, make sure it's meaningful for a good reason.

★Empty your mind: If your mind is clouded, empty it. When you need to concentrate, empty your mind. If your thoughts are full of hate, empty your mind. If you want a fresh start in life, empty your mind. Our minds are constantly preoccupied with many things. Sometimes this can prevent us from seeing and thinking clearly. On occasion, we need to erase certain thoughts that are not beneficial to us. Sometimes we need to clear our minds and start fresh.

★Rewards come as compensation for a job well done. Life is a job; perform well and do the right things. Work hard and do your best, and you will be rewarded for your effort.

★Do you know who you are? Do you know what you want? Do you know what's needed to get there? Do you have what it takes? If you don't know, who does?

★Your most challenging goal is to never stop challenging yourself.

# *Inspiration*

This category involves inspiration. It includes inspiring quotes and thoughts. While the entire story is inspiring, this part of the book tells of *my* inspiration.

Many things inspire me. Things that inspire one person may not inspire another. We all have something different that drives us. On the other hand, people have a lot of these things in common.

My mother and father were the first sources of my inspiration. After migrating from another country—literally off the boat—my mother became a homemaker in Canada, while my father worked three jobs to support my mother, sister, and myself. We moved to the United States six years later, and my father continued to work several jobs. My mother got a job at an industrial laundry corporation manufacturing clothing.

In just a few short years, my mother became a supervisor. Then she became a general manager in charge of many people. This company had twenty-five locations around the country, and she was running the corporate office. By the end of her career, my mother was traveling across the country to the other plant locations to train managers on how to run the plant more effectively. My mother stayed at this company thirty-one long years. She achieved all of this with no college education.

My father worked his tail off, and after just a few years, he had saved enough money to purchase a Laundromat. He worked his day job and also ran his business after work. We all pitched in to help. Like my mother, he did not have a college education. In those days, college was more of a luxury than a necessity. Things weren't always great. My parents managed to do whatever it took to get by and give our family what we needed to be okay. They had focus, desire, and the will to survive.

Throughout my life, and as my ailments came, I never lost sight of the fact that with desire, perseverance, and confidence, anything is possible. Many people lose sight of that on occasion; we all need to be reminded of it sometimes.

I graduated from high school wanting to become a police officer. I tried many times to achieve this goal. I took many civil service exams and passed them all. I was put on a waiting list with other qualified candidates. I never received the call; I never scored high enough on the test. After a while, I started looking for a different career. I started working at a local bank as a teller. I continued to try to become a police officer while working at the bank. I found myself actually liking the bank. I found that I really enjoyed people, customers, and helping customers. I made friends quickly with my manager, my coworkers, and—most of all—my clients. I realized real fast that this was my calling: to work in a customer service industry where I could be myself and meet other people. I realized that maybe becoming a police officer was not what I was meant to do. I was born to deal with and help others.

That all happened in 1985 when I was just twenty years old (six months before my brain tumor was discovered). When I was out for surgery, I received a lot of support from my employer. The surgery kept me out of work a few months, but my job was waiting for me when I returned. This was a huge confidence builder for me, as I loved my job. From that point on, I worked my butt off to please my employer. I also learned very quickly that I loved our clients. I liked to see them smile. They were friendly, and I enjoyed tending to their financial needs. I saw them weekly and sometimes daily. I liked seeing them happy, and I found out very quickly that customers were just like me; all they wanted was for someone to treat them like a person.

I soon learned that this wasn't "work" that I was doing at all. It was like I was put there to help people have a good day. I was put there to make people smile. I became friends with some of the clients and looked forward to seeing them weekly. Some of the customers would even look for me when they came in. That was 1985, and that love for customers and making them happy lasted my entire adult life. As of 2012, I was still in banking, employed as a branch manager and an investment licensed banker. My career went fairly smoothly for the next fifteen years. I held various roles in the bank including teller, teller supervisor, customer service representative, and collections officer, and I enjoyed all of them. One thing I noticed during my career was that—as I got older—people became less curious about my medical issues. Customers may have asked what happened to me or why I looked a certain way, but it was out of curiosity. They just didn't know and were inquiring. They were not bullying me or teasing me. Despite questions by many people, I accepted this form of questioning and didn't mind answering them.

In 1996, I applied to become a branch manager at the bank where I was employed. I interviewed but was not selected for the position. I was upset but not devastated. I knew I had experience, but I also knew there were other candidates who probably had a lot more experience than me. Still, I felt that I stood a good chance but was told that another person had been selected for the job. I was told that I was among the top three candidates but that the person selected had more experience. I asked my district manager what I was missing.

I asked his advice about the things I needed to do to put me in a position to be selected next time and not just be a runner-up. He gave me sound advice and I took it. In 1998, I was selected as branch manager of my first office. The important lesson here is that I did not give up. I learned why I wasn't selected and what things I needed to do. I listened to the advice a more experienced person had given me. He was more than happy to help. He once told me that he knew I would one day be a branch manager the moment I asked him what I needed to do to become the branch manager. He said the motivation and determination I had were exactly the qualities the bank wanted in a manager.

In 2000, I was branch manager at another office of the same bank. I had a staff of eight employees and managed a very high traffic branch with thousands of transactions per month. I began getting headaches again. I began forgetting a lot and even started having sleeping issues. I couldn't sleep at night. I would sometimes fall asleep in my car at traffic lights. I couldn't remember to do some tasks at work and sometimes did them twice. The strangest part was that I rarely realized that this was occurring. On occasion, I would vomit shortly after I ate breakfast, and at times I was disoriented. My staff brought these incidents to my attention, and at first I shrugged them off. After a few weeks, however, I went to the doctor again at my sister's insistence.

I went to my neurosurgeon. He was the same doctor who had performed my brain surgery fourteen years earlier. I was given another CAT scan. The brain tumor was normal, and there were no signs of any changes; we feared that it might have grown back. The test uncovered another problem, however. I had excess water in my brain that was causing pressure to build, which was causing my symptoms. The disorder was called *hydrocephalus*. I was told that this was ordinarily a childhood disorder. It was a serious problem that could result in serious complications; again, surgery was not only recommended but also demanded, immediately. It could kill me if surgery was not performed. Once again, and according to my neurologist, this disorder was attributed to my NF. The surgery was done the very next day, and a shunt was inserted in my brain along with a long tube that extended into my abdomen.

The shunt is a pump that allows the excess water in my brain to drain into my body when the pressure builds up. The pump would be in my head for the rest of my life. Once again, the surgery was a success. This time, I was out of work for about four months. I recovered fully and returned to my job. Again, my employer was wonderful and patient, allowing me to stay employed in my current position. I was able to receive e-mails at home to stay in touch with events happening at work. My boss at the time was a huge inspiration during my sickness and was always encouraging me to take care of myself and to come back to work when I was ready.

Each time I had a medical issue, I was supported by my family, my employer, and my friends. They encouraged me to carry on and not worry about anything. This was very inspiring and important to me in my life. I also had the determination to not let this thing defeat me. I refused to let this little water issue bring me down. After all, I had survived scoliosis, a brain tumor, and NF! This was nothing!

If there is one thing as important as others inspiring you, it's that you must also inspire yourself. Nothing can stop you if you don't let it. Something might slow you down, but only your attitude can stop you. I believe that every person is capable of success and good mental health. Good mental health means staying positive and confident and believing that you will be okay when things don't go as planned. Believing this is the key to achieving what you want. Always believe that you are strong and that you will overcome obstacles. We are all capable of making that obstacle only a temporary setback that will never prevent us from achieving success.

# Inspirational Thoughts and Quotes

*Live your life like you would if today were your last day and you wanted people to be left with the person you truly are.

*Existence: Why do we exist? Why do we do the things we do? What is our purpose? No one knows the answers for sure to any of these questions. Some may go through life and never have the answers as to why we exist. There is a purpose to every life. Love, caring, and honesty are the three main ingredients to help you find your purpose. Remember—your purpose is rarely about you.

*Greatness: We all strive for it. On occasion we achieve it. Some people don't know the ingredients to achieve greatness. We all have what it takes: drive, persistence, determination, vision, and goals. But greatness has other ingredients: heart, passion, caring, forgiveness, confidence, and—most of all—*leadership*. Only with all of this will you achieve true greatness.

*Inspire someone today. Say one kind thing to someone. Just one act of kindness makes a difference.

*Motivation: We are all motivated by different things. Life gives us many options. The only thing we need is the motivation to pursue the things we desire or the things we want to stop. Doing nothing does not help you meet that goal. We are all capable of achieving greatness. Your motivation lies within you. The result is your reward.

*Residue: It's what's left after you have been in someone's life and are no longer there. It's what's left after you have worked in the same place for thirty years and then suddenly retire. It's what happens when you suddenly leave this life unexpectedly. It's what you leave behind, what's remembered. Were you kind? Were you patient, sincere, truthful, and honest? What will people say about you after you are no longer around? Will they miss you? Did your time with them have meaning? Leaving a part of yourself with those you were with will only have meaning if it was a positive, memorable experience.

*Beauty isn't always looks. Beauty is *caring*; beauty is *personality*. Beauty is forgiving. Beauty of this type is beautiful.

*Cherish what you have, not what you don't have—or soon you will not have what you have and you will cherish what you don't have.

*Talent—it can come in many forms. Someone might have a singing talent, a dancing talent—or maybe he or she is funny or has perfect timing. Maybe he or she has a way with words, a way with fixing problems for others, or maybe he or she just has a way with pretending not to be talented in anything. Talent doesn't have to always be spectacular. Used right, it can accomplish wonders. The important thing is for people to realize their talents, and to uncover and use them. Help someone uncover his or her talent. Tell someone that he or she has talent and that person can achieve wonders.

*What's on my mind? What's not? Just do the best you can with the best you have.

*Unknown: We all live our lives knowing things will happen—things like school, work, births, deaths, graduations, marriage, divorce, and many other things that include happiness and sadness, anger, and laughter. We never truly know what fate will bring us. We can help fate by doing certain things that will help or hurt us. What we cannot understand and what we don't know is why brilliant, young, beautiful souls are taken from us unexpectedly. Why do good people who are so full of promise—or people who have been near perfect—have to pass on? The only answer is that only God knows. We need to remember these people and try to live our lives as they did. We need to keep their legacy alive by appreciating life and those in our lives.

*Imagine: That you can do what you can do when you want to. Imagine the time you would save if you stopped wasting it. Imagine how far you would get if you didn't stop short. Imagine what you could solve if you stopped fighting. Who said imagination is bad? Just *imagine* and make it happen!

*Happiness: While most of us are generally happy, some are not very happy. It's not necessarily because they aren't actually *happy*, but it's because they or someone they love are dealing with issues they are having difficulty with. Most people are used to dealing with issues in our own way, but they have a tough time dealing with loved ones' issues because they cannot control them. Your role is to be there every step of the way when friends are dealing with issues like this. Pray for them, listen to them, call them, talk to them, and again—just be there. It's your strength that will help your friends deal with their problems. Just knowing friends are there will help them deal.

*Life is an amazing journey. We are only here for a short time. All the joy, happiness, pain, and sadness are part of the trip. It's what we do and how we react to things that matter. It's the love that we show each other. It's the caring, the guidance we give, the way we treat others, and the way we behave. Lead by example, and teach our young how to behave and how to live a good life—not how to hate nor how to be selfish. Life doesn't always deal you a great hand of cards. It's up to you to teach the people you care about (and anyone else you can) that you can still win, no matter what hand you get. Staying positive and doing positive things helps you overcome negativity. Care for others and you will be cared for. In the end, you will always be part of someone's life.

*November is a time for thanks, a time for family, a time for closeness, a time for kindness, and a time of generosity. Be thankful for what you have. But wait—why do we have to wait *all year* to feel like this? Why wait to be thankful for what we have? Why wait until Thanksgiving to be with the entire family (for those who have family nearby)? Why not make Thanksgiving just another weekly or biweekly gathering with friends and family? Always be thankful for what you have. Always share your good fortune (humor, knowledge, and kindness) with others year-round.

*The only thing that matters in life is that *life matters*. Make your life meaningful.

*Inspire your friends, inspire your brothers and sisters, and inspire your coworkers. Inspire yourself, and have confidence and inner strength. You need to take care of yourself too.

*What's life without a few bumps in the road? Keep your hands on the wheel, steer straight, and you won't go off track.

*Prestige, power, fame, money, and status: If you could achieve all of this tomorrow, what would you do to get there? Hmm, think carefully. Now, if you could achieve all these things with hard work, honesty, integrity, sacrifice, and sweat—would you work as hard to get there? Or would you quit because it's too hard? True satisfaction is achieved by earning what you get.

*Always know that you are capable of endless possibilities. Trust yourself to make decisions, and don't be afraid. We all need guidance—but without risk, there is no reward.

*Fall is here, and it's time to remember that weather changes for a reason. It changes to refresh and keep life going. It changes to bring new life in the spring. The four seasons should remind you that change is good. Change happens for a reason, and change is very meaningful. The way change affects you depends on how you accept it. Accept change and refresh!

*Life is short. It goes by in the blink of an eye. Cherish every moment and always love; never hate. You may not get a second chance.

*Have the guts to do the things that others only dream of. You will inspire others to fulfill their dreams.

*Dream big and never give up. Somewhere along the way, you will find success.

*Inspire yourself and inspire others. Make someone feel special, and *you* will be special.

*Inspire: This is a very powerful word. When you inspire others, you give them a gift that is better than any gift they can ever unwrap. Inspire someone, and help fulfill someone's goal. It's easier than you think—just be *you*!

*While you are alive, remember to live. Explore, experiment, and pursue your goals. Have fun doing it. Work hard and sweat, but laugh along the way. Do not just lay waiting for something great to happen. Things come to those who pursue. Go after what you want. A little effort pays huge dividends. Work hard and be happy. Hard work doesn't have to hurt, especially if you love what you do. Find your passion.

*Peace: It's what we all want. We want inner peace. We want world peace. We just want to be happy and for things to be calm in our lives. It all begins with you. Live your life peacefully. Always treat everyone you encounter with respect. One step at a time, peace can happen.

*Raise your head up. Be proud of who you are. Set your goals high. There isn't anything that cannot be done. No one has ever accomplished a goal without heart, passion, and effort.

*Proud: Be proud of what you believe in. Be proud of your job. Be proud of your goals. Be proud of your family. Be proud of your friends. Most importantly, be proud of making the decisions to change what you're *not* proud of. We all need one or two changes to make our lives better, healthier, or happier. Recognize, change, implement—and be *proud*.

*Satisfaction is knowing that you did your best the first time, regardless of the outcome. Satisfaction is also knowing that you struggled many times—despite doing your best—before finally succeeding, regardless of the number of attempts. Always do your best. Never give up on what you truly believe in. You may not reach your goal the first time, or even the tenth time—or maybe you will—but at least you will have the satisfaction of knowing you gave it your best shot.

*Inspiring someone makes you want to inspire others. Watching the result is priceless.

*At this very moment you can change the world. The world changes every day. Are you ready to be part of the change? Always be your best. Always *think*. Always be positive. The level of your participation is up to you.

*Why be miserable?
Why be mad?
Life is wonderful.
It isn't sad.
You must have love, care, respect.
You must have goals and dreams.
It will be bigger than you expect.
Life is better than it seems.

*Fear: Do not fear anything; nothing can frighten you. Challenges should excite you, not scare you. Do not fear anything because you will win. It may take one, two, or three times—but you will never lose because fear will fear *you*.

# Confidence

This category is all about having confidence to overcome anything in your life. It's about having the confidence to believe in *you*. It's also about having the confidence to move forward with your life, regardless of any issues you may face. Confidence is very important to have in every aspect of your life.

This is a huge word for me. I was not always confident in everything I did. As a child, I was very sure that I liked people and that I could easily make friends with anyone. Unfortunately, not every person I encountered felt the same way. As an eight-year-old and a new kid in the neighborhood, I didn't know many people. I met a kid who became my friend, and his brothers also became my friends. We stayed friends for many years and are still friends forty years later.

This neighborhood had many kids in it, and they all seemed to be in groups. I was singled out and picked on from day one. I was bullied for being short, bullied for being dark-skinned, even bullied for my lunch. I never fought back. I was never very physical or aggressive. In fact, the most physical thing I did as a child was play Little League baseball for a couple of years. I didn't like fighting and didn't want to be involved in any fights. I didn't know what to do; I had never encountered this before and didn't know why these kids were being so mean. It was mostly one kid who did the bullying, and I was not the only one being picked on. This kid singled out several others and would always pick on them. I noticed that the bullying was worse when other kids were around, but when no one was around I hardly ever got picked on. This went on for a year or so, but it seemed like an eternity. This bullying had nothing to do with my NF disorder. In fact, at that point in my life I didn't even know I had it.

One day, while playing hockey with some of the neighbors, I saw the bully's older brother. We had never really talked much to each other, but we frequently played games together with the other kids. One day, we were walking back from a game and we started talking. I asked him why his brother always picked on me. He said that his brother was a mean kid and that he had been talked to before about his bullying. He said that he would speak to his brother. From that day forward his brother never picked on me again. I couldn't believe it was that easy. In fact, the bullying ended immediately. I wish I knew exactly what his brother had said to him, but whatever he said, it worked.

Over the years, the bully and I actually became friends. In fact, I became friends with the whole family. I mustered up the courage one day to ask him why he had picked on me. He said he did it because I let him. He said that I never fought back or challenged him, so he kept doing it. Hmm, what an interesting response.

My sister also played a big part in my confidence. She was always a great student in school. She went to medical school and was a district sales manager at a major air express delivery service. She raised two wonderful kids. She has always been very confident in her ability to succeed and has done just that. She also married a very successful man who is very smart and dedicated to succeeding. My sister has always been an inspiration to my confidence, showing me that anything is possible if you work hard at it. She has taught her children the same, as they are both on their way to success. One child has become an accountant, and one will graduate soon from a major broadcast journalism school. My sister's technique is a formula for success, and I have applied much of it to my life.

I have carried that confidence throughout my whole life. I learned that you are who you are and nothing can change that—except for you. I learned that people like you for who you are, although some people may like you for *what* you are, but people who truly like and respect you do so because of *who* you are. I also learned that when you are truly sincere and caring, it will show through. Most people can see that in someone. This is what life is about.

The reality of it all is this. I could have folded and succumbed to the bullying. I could have decided to do nothing about it. I used a technique that I actually didn't learn until many years later. *I asked.* I asked why he picked on me, and the answer surprised me. I let him! I never asked *him* why he was picking on me. I learned in business many years later that if you want the business, you have to ask! It's still on a rock that I have on my desk today. Always be confident and be brave. Accept that you are who you are. I applied this to my own health. I had NF, which was not by choice of course. But I had this "problem" that was actually a blessing in disguise. You see, once you establish confidence in yourself and you believe that you are who you are, your "problem" is not a problem at all. It's just part of your life. NF was part of my life. The scoliosis was part of my life. The brain tumor was part of my life. I had all these things and nothing would ever change that. So, I accepted and understood that if I were ever going to achieve success, I first needed to be confident that I *could*. A disorder like mine won't stop you from going to school or from working, and it won't stop you from achieving your goal. There may be temporary setbacks, but you carry on and move ahead with your life.

I had a heart attack when I was forty-one years old. This was completely unexpected. I had recently lost around twenty pounds and was working out with a trainer as well as dieting. That day I had an intense workout and was done for the day. I went home after my workout to enjoy my day off from work. I started feeling ill and was experiencing some shoulder pain. Suddenly, my left arm felt odd. My cousin was visiting me, and had it not been for him that day, it's possible I wouldn't be here today. He insisted that I go to the hospital, and once again I was stubborn. He persisted, however, and even though I knew he was right, I was tired and wanted to rest. He finally was able to get me up off the couch and into the car, and he drove me to the emergency room. I was transported to the hospital where I had three stents placed in my heart; luckily I had no heart damage. I had two stents placed the first day and one the next day into the more delicate part of my heart. During the surgery to place the stent, a dye was introduced into my heart to assist the doctor. My heart had a reaction to the dye and stopped beating. I was awake during the procedure, and the next thing I remember I woke up to ten doctors frantically running around my room. When I asked what had happened, I literally saw a look of fear in everyone's eyes. I was told that my heart had stopped and that they had to zap me four times! At the moment, the only thing I could say was, "Thank God you didn't stop at three times." Everyone let out a sigh of relief. When I arrived at my hospital room, the nurse started to rub this ointment on me to treat burn marks from the paddles used to zap me. Amazingly, I had absolutely no burn marks. The nurse was shocked and said that wasn't possible. It was amazing, but I really didn't have any signs of the paddles being used.

Again, I was out of work for a while. I recovered and returned to work. I was given a new lease on life. Once again, I went back to work within a couple of months and picked up where I had left off. All of my clients were very concerned about me. My coworkers and boss were worried about me. Of course, my family was worried about me too.

The previous year, I had won a corporate trip to Florida for being a top performer. This trip was awarded to the top three percent of our company's top performers in the country. NF didn't stop me from working hard. NF didn't prevent customers from coming to me for financial advice for their consumer and business needs. I also had business owners I took care of and was a licensed financial advisor who helped many clients with their investment needs. I managed a staff and we all tended to client needs. My NF had absolutely nothing to do with my abilities. My clients all saw past my disfigured face and past all the bumps on my skin and body. They saw me for *me* and most never asked a single question about what I had. My employer couldn't have cared less about my looks. They only cared about my customer service skills and my job performance. I have always performed to the best of my ability no matter what or how I was feeling. Despite all my medical ailments, I did not let my medical issues become a roadblock to my success. I was—and *am*—confident that nothing can stand in the way of your goals. I believe and can prove that you are your only roadblock. Lack of confidence is the leading cause of failure.

Since I entered the customer service industry, I have always treated people with respect. I have always smiled, laughed, joked, and listened to my clients. I was taught by my parents at a young age to look at someone when he or she talks to you. Look the person in the eyes. Always say *thank you* and *please*. When speaking to a client, I always remember to ask how he or she is doing, and I always mean it. When I speak to someone about anything, I always try to find a common ground to speak about. Sports, the weather, or life in general are great places to start. Most importantly, I always *listen* to the client and I speak less. This strategy has helped me build many friendships over the years. Many of my clients became my friends because of our relationships. Naturally, during twenty-seven years in banking, some people asked what disease or problem I had. But they were questions stemming from curiosity or because a loved one had something similar. Not *one* client that I ever waited on or took care of ever made fun of me for the way I look. Sure, on occasion while working or while out to lunch, a client might have stared or looked at me longer than normal—but this was mostly out of curiosity. If a client asked what was wrong with me, I told him or her.

The first step in building confidence is developing a rapport with people. Once you establish this, the subject matter isn't as important as the interaction. Confidence shows when speaking to others. Confidence says a lot about your character. It's much easier to sell a product to someone when you have a great relationship with the person. Believe it or not, this can be done fairly quickly.

Step two in building up confidence is getting to know what you are about to sell or talk about. See, whether you are about to speak in front of ten thousand people or are making a sales presentation to just a few people, you must know every detail about the topic before you can present it to anyone. Most importantly, you must *believe* in the product or subject. You have to believe what you are saying or you will rarely be successful. This is *confidence*, and once you learn how to use it to your advantage, almost any goal is achievable. This can be applied in your life too. If you don't believe that you can reach a certain goal and you cannot convince yourself that it can be done, then how in the world will you ever be successful? You must convince yourself before it becomes a reality. Belief builds confidence and confidence builds success.

I just celebrated my twentieth anniversary with my current employer and twenty-seven years in the same industry. There was a time when I was not always successful at work. After my surgery on my head for hydrocephalus in 2000, I returned to work. My sales numbers suffered that year because I was absent for several months. I was asked to take a step back and go to another branch while I regained my numbers and healed entirely. My office was overstaffed and the new office was understaffed. It made sense for everyone. I wasn't happy. I knew that my performance could be better, but some of it was also beyond my control. So I accepted the temporary reassignment and headed to another branch for a while.

I was determined to return to my old office to manage my staff. I set a goal for myself and reminded myself that this was numbers related and not because of my health. I fought hard and talked to every single client I knew. I told them that I had relocated and to please come see me there. I told family members that I needed help with referrals. I tried my best every time we had a sales contest at the bank. My efforts paid off. I was one of the top salespeople during that time frame and received recognition for my hard work. Prior to the end of the year, I was back in my old office as the branch manager once again. I persevered and overcame that temporary roadblock. I have endured failure and success, and success feels much better. Don't ever let the fear of failure stand in your way of being successful. It's okay to feel pain before feeling happiness.

# Confidence Thoughts and Quotes

*Be who you are, not what others want you to be. Know what this means. There are certain things in life you must do—but who you are, what you believe in, what you look like, and what your goals are should only be important to you and no one else. You need to find yourself and make mistakes along the way in order to learn what your true destiny is. We all need guidance to help us get there. But what we don't need is people who criticize, ridicule, and torment people just because they want to.

*Be happy: While there are many things to be happy about, people tend to focus on the unhappy things in life. Lots of energy is wasted and the end result is more unhappiness. Look at all the positives. There are many good things in life to be happy about. Either way, your feelings spread like wildfire. Spread happiness, not unhappiness.

*Bravery: It's following your dreams no matter what anyone tells you. It's speaking your mind to defend the defenseless. It's being aware of other people's feelings and respecting their thoughts in spite of yours. It's standing up for what you truly believe and not accepting defeat. It's being fearless to do the right thing.

*Improve: Well, where do I start? There are many things we're good at. We are better at some things—way better at other things.

We may even consider ourselves experts. So why are we so good at those things, but not so good at others? Some of those things include relationships, honesty, speaking your mind, losing weight, friendships, and teamwork. We can all improve at anything we want, but we must *want* to improve. Willpower does amazing things. At times, we should reevaluate what's important to us; we may decide to improve at some of these areas we know we have room to grow. Improve and become an expert at them. Only then will your life get better.

*Confidence: It's what you must have to do anything successfully. Sure you may be successful on occasion without it. But to be successful consistently—and efficiently—you must be confident and believe in your abilities. It's equally important to be thorough. Confidence doesn't mean a lot if you are lazy and not thorough. Confidence is built through education, positive reinforcement, and repetitive use of these techniques. Confidence builds leaders—and leaders build confidence.

*Getting ahead begins with stepping in the right direction.

*Creativity: some people are more creative than others. Some are less. Some bring creativity to a new level. Whatever your passion is, show it, work hard at it, and move at your own pace. Obstacles will get in your way; some things—or people—will try to discourage you. Those are the ones without creativity. Some people will encourage you. Listen to those people. Be creative and let your mind wander.

*Outlook: It means you have a point of view or attitude toward certain things in life—or toward the future. No one knows what the future holds. But when you have a positive outlook on things, they usually will end positively. When you have a negative outlook on things, it means you never give it a chance to be positive, so it probably won't be. Think about all the inventions we have. If the inventors had had a negative outlook after the first failed attempt, we wouldn't have most things that we have today. It works the same in your life. Have a great outlook, and you will be much happier and healthier, and you will get through life much more easily.

*Challenges will be part of your life. Overcoming challenges may *not* be part of your life. So, this is where your desire, attitude, and drive come into play. Oh, it helps to have a strong network of supportive friends and relatives. *Anyone* can overcome even the toughest challenge. The question is: Can you overcome your own inability to believe that you can overcome the challenge you are facing? *Believing* is the first step.

*Positive attitude: It helps you deal with a lot. It may not solve all your issues or problems, but it does help you through tough times. A positive attitude helps you achieve great things; it guides you through great times, too, and helps you stay on track. It keeps you optimistic and creates many other opportunities.

*Negative attitude: It does not guide you through anything but failure. It does not solve any problems. In fact, it can create additional problems. It can stop any positive progress you made earlier and can throw you off track. It makes you miserable, depressed, angry, and unfriendly. You become a pessimist in everything you do. So, when it comes to choosing attitude, the choice is positive or negative.

*Adversity: Overcoming it can truly be a challenge. But we are all capable of coping and dealing with it in our own way. What seems impossible can be achieved. What seems hopeless suddenly has hope. It all comes down to *you*. The key to handling adversity is deciding that you will not succumb to it. Your attitude, dreams, and outlook will help you overcome it.

*Your life is like a movie. It can be played and replayed in people's heads. People will remember you for your role. Never be afraid to feel, never be afraid to care, and never be afraid to love. Never forget to laugh. You will be remembered for how your life played out. Make sure your movie gets played over and over.

*Mind over matter: You can't control certain things, but you can trick those things into thinking that you *can* control them.

*Only *you* decide your future. You may have help along the way, but don't let roadblocks stop you. Go around them or plow right through them, but don't be discouraged by them.

*Attitude is king. No matter if it's negative or positive, it will decide the outcome of the situation, which could decide your future.

*Always be confident in yourself and your abilities. Always be confident you can improve. Always be confident that you control your future.

*Fear nothing: Have faith that you can overcome anything that gets in the way of your goals. You must believe, you must work hard, and you must follow through. You must be fearless.

*Always believe that you are capable of doing *anything*. Do not be afraid to challenge yourself. Even if you don't know how to do something, you will succeed. Even if you fail at first, never give up. This builds character. It may be hard, but you can do anything you need to do. You just need to *believe*.

*Never get discouraged; you can do it. Life gives you many chances to get it right. You only have to use those chances wisely. Recognize your chances, and never pass up an opportunity.

*What you desire is only within reach if you are willing to reach far enough.

*Be smart. Always think positively. Life is what you want it to be. The only person in control of your destiny is you. Think great—and it will be.

*Your mind is capable of endless tasks. Dream, imagine, create, and explore. Every single one of us has the capability to change the world.

*We all face challenges. Some of us face challenges beyond our imagination. Some find a way to overcome virtually any challenge presented to them. How? It's simple; they don't necessarily fix every problem. They adapt to some challenges and eliminate others. Either way, they control the outcome. They never let the challenge control the outcome. They learn to live happily, staying positive despite certain challenges that may or may not be permanently fixable. Challenges do not control your life; *you* do.

*Explore your mind for ways to improve your life. Get rid of all obstacles, even if you think you will miss them.

*It only takes one positive thing to set off a chain of other positive things. Positive things don't just happen. It takes someone being positive to make a positive thing happen.

*Thinking* you can succeed versus *knowing* you can succeed can make all the difference. Have confidence in yourself and your abilities. Never think that you don't have what it takes to succeed, because you *do* have what it takes.

*Visualize yourself in the future. Visualize yourself being successful. Visualize what it will take to get there. You must visualize first, then believe, and then make it happen. *Then* you will succeed.

*It's your inner strength that determines your outer weakness. Mental toughness is more powerful than physical toughness.

*Fear of failure is really the fear of success. You only truly fail if you fail to try, but success comes to you only if you try. You may have to try several times, but success is also knowing you gave it your best effort. Never be afraid to succeed. You might just find that you like it.

*Be proud of yourself, happy with yourself, and confident with yourself—because you are beautiful and you can accomplish wonders.

*Accountable: To be accountable is to take ownership. To take ownership is to be responsible. To be responsible is to be mature. Be mature; be accountable; be responsible, and take ownership.

*You are who you are. You are in control of your dreams and goals. You are in control of your present and your future. You are as powerful as you think you are. You are capable of amazing things. You will never fail if you don't allow yourself to fail. If you fail, you learn from mistakes, and try again. You will eventually succeed. Never give up. Doing your best is never failure. You are who you are.

*Think you are strong. Think you are wise. Think you are confident. Think you can accomplish any task you work hard at. Think you can achieve success. Now, replace the word *think* with *believe*. When you believe, anything is possible.

*Just when you think you can't handle any more, you find a way to handle it. Staying positive

# Health

This category is about your physical and mental health. It speaks of the importance of maintaining good health and healthy thoughts.

As I've mentioned, I have had a lot of health issues. From a brain tumor to a heart attack, I have had many medical problems—and continue to have medical issues. I have never—and *will* never—let any medical issue cloud my judgment or my mind. I refuse to let my life be dictated by things I cannot control. I have learned to relax and not worry about my health as much as some people worry. I always felt that certain things were going to happen to me that could cause health problems. I realized that if those things did happen, there were doctors who would take care of me. I put my faith in the doctors and let them do their job. I feel it is important to take care of yourself healthwise, which is something that we all (including me) need to do. I also know that worrying about things in your life that you cannot control is not healthy for your mind, body, or spirit. In fact, the less you worry about it, the quicker you heal.

One thing that goes along with health is patience. Being patient is vital to a healthy mind and body. Being calm and dealing with issues calmly helps the body and mind deal with all issues rationally. When you are told that you have a neurological disease that was a mutation and there is no cure, or told you will have growths, bumps, tumors, and many medical problems due to this disease—it will probably frighten you. No one is ever prepared for that type of news.

As a child, this is terrifying news. Then you hear that your spine is abnormal and you have months ahead of you to correct it. Then you hear that you have a brain tumor and doctors say they are unsure of the severity of this problem, but they have to do brain surgery. One day you are told you have water on the brain and the doctors have to insert a pump to drain the water. This pump has to stay in your body the rest of your life. Or you're told you have heart disease and pericardial fusion (water on the heart). These were all problems I did not cause. I was not responsible.

This information didn't all come at once; it came in short intervals. But when you hear this, your mind isn't sure what to do. Instantly, you are either going to accept that what you are hearing is real, or you are just going to nod your head and not really hear what they are telling you. So, I decided that my only option was to listen, acknowledge, and understand. The doctor knew much more about what I had than I did. He sounded very knowledgeable and confident, so I decided that he was the boss and that whatever he says goes. The only thing I knew was that I had school or a job that I had to get back to. I wasn't about to worry about myself as much as I would worry about my responsibilities. I felt confident that I was in good hands, so I immediately lost all fear about my medical issues and put my faith in my doctor's hands. Meanwhile, my mother, father, and sister had fear in their eyes. They were terrified! You would've thought it was *them* facing surgery. I showed them that I was not frightened and told them they did not need to worry. I felt good, and I wasn't afraid to proceed with any of the surgeries.

When you are calm and unafraid, your body and mind relax. Your blood pressure decreases. Your heart rate slows down. Surgery becomes easier for the doctor to perform. Your body heals better and more quickly. This is also true in life. Patience, confidence, and attitude are key to a healthy mind and body.

When I visited California in the early part of 2012, I wasn't feeling that well. I was tired and sluggish. I figured it was due to my body being overwhelmed with constantly being on the go. It was a well-deserved vacation. My neck was bothering me, and I had a little trouble walking long distances with getting tired fast. I noticed that this wasn't normal, but I thought that being on vacation would take care of it. The night I arrived back home, I was exhausted and tired. I was physically drained. I thought I had a very bad cold or some other sickness that made me feel ill. I made a doctor appointment for the very next morning.

When I went to the doctor, I was checked physically and was given an EKG. X-rays were taken, and the doctor examined me. After several hours, it was determined that I had something serious. I had fluid in my heart and heart failure. No one knew how this had happened. In fact, they checked my blood for over twenty-three things that could have caused this, only to have the findings be undetermined. I had surgery the very next day and had over two liters of fluid drained from my body. I spent nearly a week in the hospital. This condition could have eventually killed me if left untreated. I was put on steroids for several months to evaporate the water completely. This caused weight gain, but the water eventually disappeared and did not return. They never found what caused the water in my heart. I recovered fully from this as well. Again, I never doubted that I would recover. I knew I would get treated and that my doctors would do the best they could.

Many things affect your health. Your mind-set, being positive, your physical health, and your desire and belief that you will be okay are also important. These are proven factors that are critical to the outcome of nearly any health issue. The health of your mind is just as important as the health of your body. Together, overcoming health issues and dealing with them becomes easier and more bearable. Some health issues are tougher to deal with than others, but applying these tactics can make the situation more tolerable and bearable. Always focus on the health of your mind, which will help determine the outcome of the health of your body.

NF affects those of us who have it differently, and it can cause many other medical issues. The severity of problems associated with having it depends on an individual's body. No one knows what it's like to have a disease, except for the person who has it. No one can live that person's life. But people with a medical disorder can help guide, inspire, and remind others with a disease that our ultimate destiny is in our hands. NF will not control our lives. *We* will control NF.

# Healthy Thought Quotes

*Take care of your health. Do what you have to do to be healthy and happy. Nothing is more important than your health. In the end, this determines many other things.

*Please try to enjoy your night. It will make for a better day tomorrow.

*Relaxing: It's highly underestimated and unappreciated. Your body needs it. It needs sleep. It also needs to just do nothing sometimes. The nice part about this is that it also gives you time to be with your family and spend quality time with them—or even quiet time with friends. It gives you time to think, to dream, to refresh, and to just be you. When we have tons of things going on in our lives, it becomes hectic and stressful and it builds up. Keeping busy is good, but you need to find time to relax; you may uncover that dream you never knew you had.

*Create your story: write it page by page, day by day. Will it be a best seller? Will it be fiction, nonfiction, drama, or romance? Will it involve truth and honesty—or lies and deception? Whether it's a memorable book or not depends on the story. Make sure your book is remembered for the right reasons. Make sure it gets read many years after you're gone.

*Remember when? Remember the good old days? Remember when things were cheaper? Remember that old friend? Remember when you were lighter? Remember when things were easier? Well, the past is behind you. Focus on today. Make it count. The present will become tomorrow's past. Make those memories great.

*Move forward, not backward. Look for opportunities to improve your life. Never settle for second best. Always respect people you encounter. Success isn't always about what you have. It's about who you are.

*Good health is a very important part of our lives. Without it, we suffer—and our loved ones suffer. Strong will and positive thoughts and prayers from those who love us help tremendously. Don't ever take your health for granted. Get regular check-ups and don't smoke. Most importantly, have faith in God that you will get through this with the help of great doctors and medicine. As always, stay positive. It's the best medicine.

*I am watching football. I'm hanging with friends later. I will probably play cards. I am thinking of going grocery shopping. I am going to do a load of laundry. I am not complaining about people who piss me off. I am not being miserable. I'm not blaming others for my feeling mad or bad. I'm not making excuses. Our lives contain many things that happen in the course of the day. Some is good news and some is not so good. Never dwell on the negative. Don't worry about things you can't control. Never make excuses. Live your life and be positive. *No excuses!*

*No matter what you do, no matter who you are, no matter how you look, no matter how you feel, no matter what you think—*you matter.*

*Smile and be happy. Every day you can smile is another day that you live. Frown and be mad. Every day that you frown or are mad is a day that you aren't able to live.

*Being miserable is not healthy. Blaming others for misery is useless. Focus on happiness. Blame someone for your happiness, this is healthy. Life should not be wasted. Make the best of it.

*When you're sad, make someone smile. You will feel better. When you're happy, show it with kindness to those who are sad.

*Spring is in the air. March madness is among us! Spring is a time for a fresh start. Nature refreshes; we can refresh too. Put all your bad habits behind you and start over. Restart your life *today*.

*Realize: Realize what it means to be living the way we live. Realize why things happen the way they happen. Realize when you're feeling happy and appreciate it. Realize when you're sad and accept it; sadness will happen. Realize that many things that happen to you are within your control. Realize that you exist for a reason. Realize your purpose and *live it*.

*Inner peace: It's when you have strength and confidence. It's when you have a positive outlook and a positive attitude. It's when you have a good, strong character. It's when you can close your eyes at night and know that you can live with the day you just lived. It's when you are honest and caring. When you possess these traits, nothing stands in your way. Nothing can defeat you. Opportunities are endless.

*Where does our soul reside? Does it live in our brain? Does it live in our heart deep inside? The question may drive you insane.

*It makes no difference where the soul hides. It only matters that our soul is alive—full of care and love inside. Even at death, our soul survives.

*Relax: Relaxation comes to all who wait for it. Work for your turn and wait for your right to relax.

*Feeling the wind blow means you are alive. Be thankful you can feel it.

*Longevity: If you want your career or relationship to last a long time, you must not only enjoy whom you are with or what you do, but you must also accept change and adapt to it. You must be willing to do things you may not agree with. You must stay enthusiastic about your job or relationship and feel fortunate that you even have one. But most of all, you must *want* longevity, or it will never happen.

*Laughter is truly an important part of life. Finding humor in everyday situations is simple. Laughing allows the mind to take a break from stressful things. Be serious about your future, but don't forget to laugh along the way.

*A friend doesn't need sympathy or a solution. A friend needs you to listen and to not judge.

*We are one and we are together—no more hate, no more anger. It's time to live together with one goal in mind: our children's future. Teach love, caring, and selflessness. This is not unrealistic; this is a *must*. It's time for adults to stop putting themselves ahead of their children.

*Enjoy life; it is precious. Always be positive and pleasant. Appreciate the things you have and appreciate that you have the opportunity to better your life. Always do your best.

*Truth is always the right path to take in life. Always care for others even if they don't seem to care for you; it's possible that no one has ever cared for them before. Money, fame, and status have little meaning without honesty and caring.

*Where are you going? It's okay to ask for directions, but you will have to make the final decisions.

\*Hardship is *strength* in disguise.

\*Feel strong and be strong. Dream big and dream often.

\*Your mental health depends on your mental attitude. Caring is healthy; loving is healthy. Having a positive attitude is healthy. Being confident is healthy. Believing in yourself and your capabilities builds self-esteem, which is very healthy.

\*Laughter is good. It makes us smile. It helps us cope with life. It reminds us that we can still enjoy the day and that there is good in all of us. Sometimes we even have to laugh at ourselves. Take time to laugh. It might be the healthiest thing you've done in a while.

\*Heart: This could have a couple of meanings. Heart means drive, attitude, desire, and passion in everything you do. Heart also means being loving and caring, always being compassionate and sincere, and always putting others ahead of yourself. But all this will mean nothing if you don't take care of your heart. Do whatever it takes to stay healthy and take care of your body. Without a healthy heart, we cannot teach others how to have heart.

# Conclusion

By now you know about the things I've endured and the messages I have to give. I strongly believe in every single thought and message I have written. Some may say that I have suffered throughout my life; I don't see it that way. I feel that I have been very fortunate to have people who have cared for me—and to have people whom I have cared for. I am fortunate to have had the love and support of my family and friends over the years, and that can never be taken from me. I have a spirit and a character that cannot be broken, no matter the situation. Despite my medical problems, I have had a good career, and I believe that anyone can achieve the same results if they believe in themselves.

I care for people and I always put the feelings of others ahead of my own. Just that by itself can help to create a healthy mind and heart. I believe that anyone is capable of great things and that we are all capable of overcoming difficult times in our lives. Our future cannot always be controlled, but we can control the end result and how it affects us. Your success does not depend on whether you tried and failed or tried and succeeded.

Your success depends on the path you follow to get there, the way you react, and the confidence you have. Hardship builds character. Without it, you cannot effectively overcome current or future issues. But hardship is only an obstacle if you allow it to be one. Always believe in your own capabilities to accomplish anything in life. We are given a natural-born ability to find our own way. The path you take is up to you. Believe in yourself always, and life will present many more opportunities. Success is an ongoing task. The definition of success in one year may be different for you in the following year. Whether in life or business, ambition is always a positive trait to have. Without it, we are lost.

Mental success is far more powerful than monetary success. Always follow your heart, and your mind will lead you to happiness. The problem with the world today is that people forget how to love, how to care, and how to have fun. This can still be done while being a productive, responsible person. Caring, the mind, inspiration, confidence, and health are the most important elements in determining your life. If one can achieve these things, then anything is possible.